IN GOD'S HOUSE

Chaleta Paige-Williams

Illustrations by Javaughn Paige

WestBow Press books may be ordered through booksellers or by contacting:

WestBow Press
A Division of Thomas Nelson & Zondervan
1663 Liberty Drive
Bloomington, IN 47403
www.westbowpress.com
1 (866) 928-1240

Because of the dynamic nature of the Internet, any web addresses or links contained in this book may have changed since publication and may no longer be valid. The views expressed in this work are solely those of the author and do not necessarily reflect the views of the publisher, and the publisher hereby disclaims any responsibility for them.

Any people depicted in stock imagery provided by Getty Images are models, and such images are being used for illustrative purposes only.
Certain stock imagery © Getty Images.

Interior Image Credit: Javaughn Paige
Cover Image Credit: Javaughn Paige

Scripture taken from the King James Version of the Bible.

ISBN: 978-1-9736-9739-8 (sc)
ISBN: 978-1-9736-9738-1 (e)

Library of Congress Control Number: 2020913144

Print information available on the last page.

WestBow Press rev. date: 08/28/2020

WestBow
PRESS®
A DIVISION OF THOMAS NELSON
& ZONDERVAN

This book is dedication to our Lord and Savior Jesus Christ for giving me the vision to share the gospel. I'd also like to thank my loving family for all of your support. A special thank you to my Father for teaching me the meaning of unconditional love and to my Mother for showing me how to never give up.

Exodus 20:8

Remember the sabbath day, to keep it holy.

On Sunday morning, we go to Sunday school.

Proverbs 1:5

A wise man will hear, and will increase learning; and a man of understanding shall attain unto wise counsels:

In Sunday school, we learn about God.

Psalms 25:4

Shew me thy ways, O LORD;
teach me thy paths.

We play with puzzles and games.

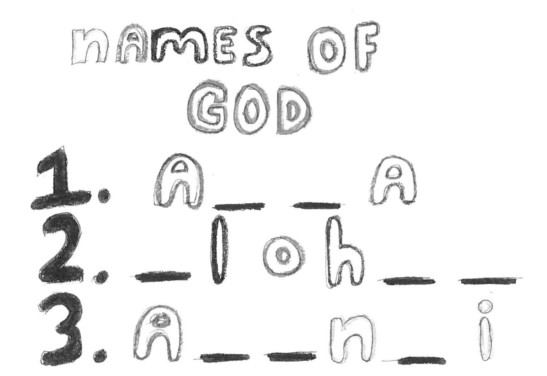

NAMES OF
GOD
1. A _ _ _ A
2. _ l o h _ _ _
3. A _ _ _ n _ i

1) Abba
2) Elohim
3) Adonai

Psalms 67:3

Let the people praise thee, O God; let all the people praise thee.

We sing songs of praise.

Psalms 98:4

Make a joyful noise unto the Lord, all the earth: make a loud noise, and rejoice, and sing praise.

After Sunday school, we go to chapel.

John 4:24

God is a spirit: and they that worship him must worship him in spirit and in truth.

Again, we pray, we sing songs, and we read God's Word.

Matthew 21:22

And all things, whatsoever ye shall ask in prayer, believing, ye shall receive.

We fold our hands and pray.
When we pray, we talk to God.

Psalms 95:6

O come, let us worship and bow down: let us kneel before the Lord our maker.

Mommy says that God always hears our prayers. God must be awfully busy!

Lord,
    thank you for
    mommy and
    Daddy
                    Amen

Psalms 33:13-14

The Lord looketh from heaven; he beholdeth all the sons of men. From the place of his habitation he looketh upon all the inhabitants of the earth.

Mommy sometimes waves her hands.
Sometimes she cries tears of joy!
She may even stomp her feet.

Psalms 96:9

O worship the Lord in the beauty of holiness: fear before him, all the earth.

We want to show God how much we love him.

Matthew 4:9

And saith unto him, All these things will I give thee, if thou wilt fall down and worship me.

Mommy says that God is everywhere and that he watches over us. We must try our best to be good boys and girls.

Psalms 125:4

Do good, O LORD, unto those that be good, and to them that are upright in their hearts.

Genesis 24:26

And the man bowed down his head, and worshipped the Lord.

Psalms 132:7

We will go into his tabernacles:
we will worship at his footstool.

About the Author

The author Chaleta Paige-Williams decided to write "In God's House" about twenty-three years ago for her two year old daughter Chaleah. She searched various bookstores, libraries, and retail stores looking for a children's book that shared their unique Christian experience. As a single mother she raised her five children in Canal Winchester, Ohio a small town outside of Columbus, Ohio. She and her children were active members of the Church of Christ of the Apostolic Faith then later New Birth Christian Ministries. She hope that you and her five young grandchildren will enjoy her story. The illustrations were created by her oldest son Javaughn Paige when he was eleven years old.